THE MAFIA COOKBOOK

PUBLISHED BY BE THE ROCK PRESS

First published 1988

Third Edition

All recipes credited to Tony La Rocco, Jr.
chef, epicurean and entrepreneur

Publisher	Barbara La Rocco
Cover	Pat Redding Scanlon
Illustrations	Scott Dutton
Print Setup	Sue Caufield
Cover Photo	Anthony La Rocco (108th Street Gang)

La Rocco, Barbara

The mafia cookbook / Barbara La Rocco

ISBN 978-0-9729803-4-0

Available as an electronic book: ISBN 9798330566303

1. Cookery, Italian. 2. Mafia--United States--Humor. I. Title.

THE MAFIA COOKBOOK

KILLER RECIPES FROM GANGLAND KITCHENS

Barbara La Rocca

In loving memory of Tony La Rocco, Jr.
and Uncle "Banana" Mike, who knew
that life is like a plate of spaghetti —
sometimes messy, always better with a
splash of good wine, and best enjoyed
with a side of hearty laughter!

CONTENTS

Part 1
STARTERS

OPEN-SEASON ANTIPASTO

The mob declared open season on Benjamin "Bugsy" Siegel for refusing to repay money he borrowed to finance the Flamingo Casino in Las Vegas. Siegel is credited with saying, "We only kill each other." Bugsy's old partner in crime Meyer Lansky cooked up the vendetta and the hit was made at the home of Siegel's mistress Virginia Hill.

1 head of romaine lettuce
1 hard-boiled egg
2 artichoke hearts
½ lb. prosciutto
½ lb. capicolli
pepperoncini
1 large tomato
2 anchovy fillets
2 celery sticks
½ lb. salami
½ lb. provolone cheese

For da nefarious nibbler ... anyting goes, and before you know it you're up to youse elbows in it. Feather your nest wid a border of romaine lettuce and sliced tomatoes. Da tip-off is prosciutto, salami, capicolli, and provolone cheese. Garnish wid one hard-boiled egg, anchovy fillets, artichoke hearts, celery, and pepperoncini.

VEGETABLE VENDETTA

Prepare with a vengeance to cause "agata," *or indigestion, in your foe. Mob triggermen believed that rubbing the tips of bullets in garlic caused gangrene in their victims.*

assortment of raw vegetables
6 tbs. unsalted butter
5 tbs. olive oil
1 can anchovies, drained
6 chopped garlic cloves

Da perfect accomplice to raw vegetables. A potent, buddery, garlic flavored hot sauce. Trow all da ingredients in a medium saucepan and put da heat on for 15 minutes. Lay out da raw vegetables, anyting youse like, on a tray and use da sauce for a dip.

DA HOT SKINNY

The mob painted the town red on the "Night of Sicilian Vespers," which was a bloody war to dominate the country's crime families. The hit on boss Sal Maranzano sparked the violence. Sal wanted to be the "boss of bosses" and was disposed of with six stab wounds, four bullets, and a slit throat.

2 large eggplants
2 tbs. cider vinegar
4 tsp. chopped garlic
1 cup Niçoise olives
2 tbs. toasted pine nuts
olive oil
8 cherry tomatoes
4 eggs
2 cups breadcrumbs
4 tbs. fresh chives
salt and pepper

Youse peel and cut da eggplant inta long, thin slices, da dimensions of da nozzle of a .45 Magnum. Sprinkle wid salt and pepper on both sides. Beat up da eggs and douse eggplant pieces. Den coat wid breadcrumbs and trow da eggplant inta hot oil in batches. Brown and drain. Dump da vinegar in a deep dish; add eggplant and top wid garlic. Fuggedaboudit for four hours. Bounce da garlic. Lay vegetables wid da eggplant on a platter and sprinkle wid pine nuts and chives.

CAPO-NATA

In the Mafia, most wise guys are soldiers. The Capo, or under-boss, reports directly to the top and relishes the boss's position.

2 medium eggplants
1 clove garlic
3 stalks celery, diced
4 bell peppers
6 oz. pitted olives
2 tbs. dried basil
1 tbs. celery salt
½ cup olive oil
3 tbs. sugar
3 cups red wine vinegar
1 large onion, chopped
2 plum tomatoes, chopped
¾ tsp. oregano
salt and pepper

Peel da eggplant and chop up wid a sharp blade. Simmer da onion, celery, and garlic in oil until tender. Trow in eggplant, tomato, bell peppers, and da olives. Cook uncova'd for 10 minutes. Add sugar, seasonings, and vinega. Simmer additional 25 minutes, den put on ice ova night. Serve wid hot garlic bread.

PATRIARCA PUFFS

Raymond Patriarca, boss of the New England crime syndicate, ran his extensive illicit operations from the National Cigarette Company offices in Providence, Rhode Island. Convicted and sentenced to jail for armed robbery, Ray received a pardon from the governor. The pardon was attributed to a puffy letter from one Father Fagan begging leniency on the mobster's behalf. It turned out that the letter-writing priest did not exist.

1 stick butter
1 cup flour
1½ tsp. salt
½ tsp. pepper
4 eggs
¾ cup Gruyère cheese
¾ cup Parmesan cheese
salad oil

Boil budda in a cuppa water. Take da heat off. Trow da flour, salt, and pepper in da pot and beat wid a wooden spoon until blended. Set ova medium heat 'til da mixture pulls away from da sides of da pot. Make da switch to a bowl and add eggs, one at a time. Add da cheeses and beat repeatedly. Form inta puffs and deep fry at 350°F until brown. Drain.

DA BIG CHEESE

Mozzarella has long been king with the mob. The "whey" of this cheesy business was to milk dry New England dairies.This caused utter confusion in the ill-fated industry. The Mafia sank its teeth into the cheese industry by practicing their first law of profit: If you don't pay your overhead, your gross is net.

3 eggs
1½ lbs. mozzarella
2 cups breadcrumbs
2 cups flour
vegetable oil
dash of salt

Youse heat plenty of oil in a deep pan. Beat tree eggs wid salt. Slice da mozzarella inta finger-size pieces. Roll da cheese in flour. Dip in beaten egg, roll in breadcrumbs, and den dip back in da egg again. Put da drop on da cheese in da oil. Pull out when golden brown and drain. Serve wid some marinara sauce.

GENOVESE MINESTRONE

As with all traditional dishes, recipes may vary from family to family. During Vito Genovese's reign as boss of the New York crime family founded by Lucky Luciano, goombah gourmets dared serve no other. When don Vito fell for a married dame, her husband fell hard. The mobster had the husband of his girl tossed off a rooftop, thus freeing up the dame to become his wife.

1 ham bone
2 carrots, diced
2 tbs. pesto
1 tsp. basil
1 onion, chopped
1 tsp. parsley
Parmesan cheese
3 celery stalks, chopped
½ head cabbage, shredded
7½ cups beef broth
1 garlic clove, chopped
1 small squash, diced
1 potato, diced
orzo (rice-shaped noodles)

Trow da ham bone in a saucepan wid onion, carrot, celery, cabbage, beef broth, and pesto. Bring to a boil and skim off any scum dat rises. Simmer for tree hours. Add water if soup gets too thick. Add squash, potato, and garlic. Simmer for 20 more minutes. Add orzo and simmer until da pasta is cooked ta da tooth (al dente). Stir in basil and parsley. Serve hot wid Parmesan cheese.

PESTO ("TO CRUSH")

During the Allied invasion of Italy in World War II, Vito Genovese helped the U.S. military crush black market rings—he was a translator and facilitator. Then, he used his own boys as heroin exporters and arms dealers. Meanwhile, he was wanted in the United States for the murder of a gangster named Ferdinand Boccia. Genovese was arrested and sent back to the U.S. where he was acquitted of the crime because the only witness was poisoned.

1 cup fresh basil
2 garlic cloves, chopped
¼ cup pine nuts, chopped
½ cup Parmesan, grated
3 tbs. olive oil
salt

In a large mortar, add da basil, garlic, pine nuts, Parmesan cheese, and a heavy shake of salt. Pound wid da handle of a pistol until thick and pasty. Work in olive oil a drop at a time until da mixture is buddery smooth.

GUM-SHOE GUMBO

New Orleans' police chief Peter Hennessey stumbled upon the existence of America's first powerful Mafia faction. He was murdered in 1890 for investigating the secret society. Hennessey's murder sparked public outrage. Angry citizens broke into city jails and lynched nine of the men associated with the murder. Italy demanded and received a formal apology from the city of New Orleans.

1 stew chicken
2 cups flour
½ cup olive oil
2 tomatoes, skinned
1 cup fresh okra
1 bell pepper, chopped
1 small onion, diced
½ tsp. salt
¼ cup rice
5 cups water

Youse break da bones of da chicken and pull it apart. Dredge da pieces wid flour and brown 'em in a saucepan of hot olive oil. Add 4 cups of boiling water and simmer until da meat falls offa da bones. Drain stock and reserve. Trash da bones and chop up da meat. Trow meat in a small pot and add tomatoes, okra, bell peppers, onion, salt, and rice. Dump in da stock, simmer 20 minutes. If da soup thickens, add water. Cook until da vegetables are tender.

GODFATHER GAZPACHO

Frank "Funzi" Tieri epitomized the Godfather image. Like the fictional don Corleone, Tieri spoke in a raspy whisper. The U.S. government's case against Funzi was the first to hold the head of a crime family accountable for the dirty deeds committed by its members in the name of the family.

2 large tomatoes
3 tbs. lemon juice
1 cucumber, diced
1 garlic clove
1½ tsp. salt
½ cup mixed herbs: chives, basil, parsley, tarragon, chervil
1 Spanish onion
1 bell pepper
½ cup olive oil
½ tsp. paprika
breadcrumbs
3 cups water

Peel and seed da bell pepper and tomatoes. Trow in a blender wid all da udda stuff. Add tree cupsa water and liquify. Put on ice and fuggedaboudit for four hours. Sprinkle breadcrumbs on top and serve.

Part 2
DA PIZZA CONNECTION

DA DOUGH

The Mafia's control of the mozzarella cheese industry and the informal nature of bookkeeping in the pizza business made it an easy mark for mob control. The syndicate used their pizza connection to traffic heroin throughout the country even though the old-time mafioso strongly opposed mob involvement in the drug trade.

¼ oz. yeast **3 cups flour** **1 tsp. salt**

Youse dissolve da yeast in ¾ cuppa warm water. Fuggedaboudit for ten minutes. Sift togedda tree cupsa flour wid salt. Stir up wid da yeast and trow in anudda ½ cuppa warm water until it forms a soft dough. Knead da dough for five minutes. Trow da dough in a greasy bowl and wait 'til it rises.

Punch da dough when it doubles in volume and knead again. Divy out da dough inta six balls. Follow recipe for Sicilian or Neapolitan pizza.

COUNTERFEIT PLAY DOUGH

Do not eat! Play and mold your own "family."

3 cups flour
1½ cups salt
3 tbs. cream of tartar
3 tbs. oil
1 cup water
1 tbs. food coloring

Mix up all da stuff. Heat and stir 'til youse can't stir no more. Cool off and knead 'til da dough is consistent. Separate inta tree portions and add food coloring to tint each portion. Store it ina plastic bag.

NEAPOLITAN PIZZA

"Health to all Neapolitans and death and destruction to all Sicilians!" This was the cry of young thugs kept out of the Mafia's rank and file. The older mafioso, called Mustache Petes, firmly believed in keeping the membership strictly Sicilian. In 1931, the Castellamarese War eliminated the Mustache Petes and opened the membership to non-Sicilians.

½ cup olive oil
¼ tsp. oregano
¼ tsp. pepper
½ tsp. salt
½ cup Parmesan, grated
1 cup mozzarella, sliced
1 cup marinara sauce (see da cuva up, page 40)
5 fresh basil leaves

Follow da dough recipe (page 24). Roll out dough ball inta a six-inch circle. Wid youse two hands, pick up da circle and work it from undaneath, moving it around on youse palms. Lay it on a greasy baking sheet and pinch da edges up. Brush wid olive oil.

Wid a ladle, spread marinara sauce ova da dough. Youse start in da center and work youse way out. Sprinkle wid oregano, salt, and pepper. Divy out Parmesan cheese ova da dough and top wid mozzarella cheese and basil leaves. Don't be stingy wid da cheese. Add any udda toppings you want. Bake on oiled baking sheet at 450°F for 10 minutes.

SCAR-FOCCACIA

Scarface, *the 1932 Howard Hawks movie starring Paul Muni, borrowed its title from Al Capone's nickname in order to increase ticket sales. Capone's scar and nickname date back to his juvenile delinquent days as a bartender at the Harvard Inn on Coney Island. Capone got fresh with the wrong dame. Frank Gallucio, brother of the broad, slashed the bartender's face. There is honor among crooks. Capone later hired Frank to be his bodyguard.*

¼ oz. yeast
2 tbs. olive oil
2¾ cups flour
1 tsp. sugar
¾ tsp. salt
cornmeal

Use da dough recipe (page 24), only dissolve da yeast wid sugar in warm water. Roll da ball of dough inta four rounds ¼ inch thick on a floured surface. Sprinkle a baking sheet wid cornmeal and slide da round onta da sheet. Drizzle wid olive oil and seasonings. Bake on da bottom rack of a 350°F oven for 20 minutes 'til done.

SICILIAN PIZZA

M.A.F.I.A. stands for "Morte Ala Francia Italia Anela!" *The slogan means "Death to all French is Italy's cry!" During French control of Sicily, the Mafia began as an anti-French movement and grew to be the island's dominating force.*

2 onions, chopped
½ cup olive oil
¼ tsp. oregano
1 cup Parmesan cheese
1 cup mozzarella cheese
¼ tsp. basil
1 cup marinara sauce (see da cuva up, page 40)
salt and pepper

Follow da dough recipe (page 24). Divide da dough in four parts. Roll each part inta a thick square. Slide da square onta a greasy baking sheet. Pinch da sides ta form a collar. Brush wid olive oil and ladle on marinara sauce. Top wid everyting. Bake at 450°F until da dough browns, about 15 minutes.

BEAT DA WRAP

Joe Bonanno was a jack of all trades. One of his higher profile occupations was that of funeral parlor owner. This proved a convenient line of work for a gangster and Bonanno displayed creative flare in his work. He invented the duplex coffin in which a mob stiff could be stashed under another corpse.

1 lb. Italian sweet sausage
½ lb. mozzarella, grated
¾ cup ricotta cheese
olive oil
1 egg
2 tsp. basil
salt and pepper
cornmeal
2 cups marinara sauce (see da cuva up, page 40)
4 oz. Parmesan cheese, grated

Youse makes da dough (page 24). Den youse cook up da sausage in olive oil. Cool and chop da sausage inta ½ inch pieces. Pistol-whip da egg wid one tablespoon a water. Cut up da dough inta four portions and roll inta ¼ inch thick rounds. Divy out da sausage and cheeses, includin' some ricotta cheese, to cuva half of each round. Season and fold ova. Press da edges wid a fork to seal. Brush wid olive oil. Sprinkle a little cornmeal on a baking sheet and place da wrap ina 475°F oven for 12 minutes.

Part 3

PASTA PARANOIA

PASTA PARANOIA

Always hospitable, the mob usually offered their victim food before execution. Aging Dons—suffering from the Last Supper Syndrome, a fear of getting bumped off at their favorite restaurant—are opting to cook their pasta at home. Home cooking might have added years to the lives of Joey Gallo, Carmine Galante, and Paul Castellano, to name a few.

1½ cups flour **1 tsp. salt**
1 egg **1 tbs. olive oil** **5 tbs. hot water**

Youse sift da flour wid da salt in a large bowl. Dig a well in da middle. Put da drop on da egg inta da well. Add oil and hot water. Do da job to da dough wid youse fingertips. Trow it on a floured surface and knead until it stops sticking to youse fingers. Split da dough.

Cuva da work area wid a floured tea towel. Take halfa da dough and roll it out. Spread it as thin as possible. Stretch it and pull it until you can see trew da dough. Roll da dough up loosely and cut inta slices, ¼ inch thick. Open up each slice and drape ova da back of a chair. Let da noodles dry for tirty minutes. Repeat wid da rest of da dough.

Da dough can also be shaped inta ravioli (see Ravenite ravioli, page 33). To cook, boil five to seven minutes.

RAVENITE RAVIOLI

The Ravenite Social Club, at 247 Mulberry Street in New York's Little Italy, was one of the many clubs from which the Mafia controlled their rackets. Formerly called the Alto Knights Social Club, it was renamed the Ravenite by mob boss Carlo Gambino in honor of his favorite poem, Edgar Allan Poe's "The Raven." Bugs in the club indicted John Gotti in 1992. The old club was shut down and gutted soon after.

3 oz. spinach purée
¼ cup ricotta cheese
¼ cup Parmesan, grated
salt and pepper
½ egg, beaten
1¼ tbs. flour
1 tsp. butter
nutmeg

Practice pasta paranoia (page 32). Divide da dough in two and roll out each portion very thin. Combine spinach purée, cheeses, egg, flour, melted budda, and seasonings ina bowl. Lay out one section of da dough ona floured surface and brush wid water. Place a small heap of filling on each two-inch square of dough. Loosely lay da second layer of dough ova da top. Stamp out ravioli wid a biscuit cutter. Dust wid flour. Drop da ravioli in boiling salted water. It's done when dey float.

"MADE" MACARONI

An initiate in the Mafia is known as a "made man," meaning he has it made. During the rites of entry, a gun and a knife are placed before the wise guy to signify that he is to live by the gun and the knife. And he is to die by the gun and the knife. This dish requires only a fork.

1 lb. macaroni noodles
¼ cup butter
2 cups milk
1 cup Parmesan, grated
3 tbs. flour
2 tbs. butter flakes

Cook macaroni accordin' to package instructions. Melt da budda ina skillet. Stir in flour and let simmer two minutes. Dump a cuppa macaroni water and milk in da skillet. Cook 'til it tickens. Stir in ¾ cup of Parmesan cheese and season wid salt and pepper. Trow it all togedda in a baking dish. Stir. Don't break da noodles. Sprinkle ¼ cup of Parmesan cheese and da budda flakes ova da top. Bake at 350°F for tirty minutes.

PAESAN PASTA

Giuseppe "Joe the Boss" Masseria's appetite for power was equal to his passion for pasta. Joe's last supper was with his paesan, Lucky Luciano, at Nuovo Villa Tammaro on Coney Island. The meal consisted of antipasto, linguini with clam sauce, lobster fra diavolo, cream puffs, and a quart of Chianti. Host Luciano was washing his hands in the bathroom when triggermen Vito Genovese, Bugsy Siegel, Joe Adonis, and Albert Anastasia executed the hit, stilling Joe's appetite for good.

½ cup butter
¼ cup salad oil
3 garlic cloves, minced
2 cans minced clams
¼ cup parsley
Parmesan cheese, grated
¼ tsp. dried basil
¼ tsp. dried oregano
¼ tsp. salt
1 pkg. linguini
pepper

Melt da budda and oil togedda ina saucepan. Turn da heat up. Sauté da minced garlic and clams for tree minutes. Trow da seasonings and a dash of pepper inta da pan. Simmer for 10 minutes. Cook da pasta accordin' to package instructions. Plate up, add da sauce, and sprinkle wid grated Parmesan cheese.

MANI-GOTTI

Renowned Godfather John Gotti once said, "All my talent's in my trigger finger." Gotti's rise to the top of the Gambino crime family could be traced in a trail of blood. He went from being called the Dapper Don to the Teflon Don after beating conviction three times. In 1992, he was finally convicted of RICO (Racketeer Influenced and Corrupt Organizations Act) charges and sentenced to life without parole. A combination of wire taps, the turncoat "Sammy the Bull" Gravano, and Gotti's own arrogance that sealed this fate. On June 10, 2002, at the age of 61, he died in prison from head and neck cancer.

8 oz. manicotti noodles
½ lb. sweet sausage
1 lb. ricotta cheese
1 egg
1 tsp. parsley
½ tsp. garlic salt
¼ tsp. basil
4 oz. mozzarella cheese

Boil da pasta 'til al dente. Break up da sausage and brown it. Beat da egg and trow it in wid da seasonings. Stir in ricotta cheese. Stuff cheese mixture in da noodles. Lay out ina baking dish. Cuva da noodles wid marinara sauce and mozzarella cheese. Zotze in da microwave for seven minutes.

ZITI ALLA COPPOLA

The diary of Ann Coppola detailed her hubby's nefarious activities and helped convict him. The certainty that "Trigger Mike" Coppola had killed his first wife sparked Ann's note-taking. The belief that he was supplying her daughter with drugs caused Ann to turn the diary over to police. Trigger Mike was convicted of tax evasion but served little time. Ann's suicide note read, "Mike Coppola, someday, somehow, a person or God or the Law shall catch up with you, you yellow-bellied bastard. You are the lowest and biggest coward I have had the misfortune to meet." Her request to have her ashes scattered over Coppola's home was not granted.

½ lb. bacon or pancetta
½ cup white wine
½ cup Parmesan cheese
salt and pepper
1 onion, chopped
3 eggs
1 tbs. butter
1 lb. penne noodles

Cook da bacon in budda until crisp. Keep two tablespoons of da drippings to sauté da onions. Add some wine to da onions and cook 'til it reduces by half. Chop up da bacon. Add bacon to onion togedda wid tree beaten eggs, some more wine, and da Parmesan cheese. Season to taste. Boil da pasta ina large pot of salted water 'til al dente. Drain and add pasta to da pan with sauce. Stir. Serve it while it's hot.

FRATIANNO'S FETTUCCISM

As a star witness for the feds, "Jimmy the Weasel" Fratianno pursued his vendetta against the mob with a fetish. He recalled illicit memories about his "amici nostri" *(friends of ours) in order to avoid the contract out on him. In his eight years in the Witness Protection Program, Jimmy the Weasel ran up $500,000 in bills which included a facelift, breast implants, and capped teeth for his babe. He wrote his autobiography,* The Last Mafioso, *before Alzheimer's disease rubbed out his memory for good in 1979.*

2 lbs. fettuccine noodles
3½ tsp. chicken base
1 tbs. olive oil
1 lb. butter
1 cup Parmesan cheese
1 cup ricotta cheese
1 tsp. chives, chopped
1 tsp. basil, chopped
1 cup heavy cream

Cook da fettuccine wid tree teaspoons chicken base and oil in da water. Ina saucepan, melt da budda wid da Parmesan cheese. Keep it stirred up ova medium heat. Add ricotta cheese, chives, basil, cream, and da rest of da chicken base. Youse better keep stirring. Gently coat da pasta wid sauce so's not to break any noodles.

LUCKY LASAGNA

In America, it was Charlie "Lucky" Luciano who put the "organized" in crime. He picked up the nickname "Lucky" after being the only known survivor of a one-way ride. A member of the Five Points Gang, Luciano rose to control much of New York's underworld activities. He carved up New York City, and the nation, into manageable family-run areas and structured the "Honorable Society" like a modern company with layers of command.

1 pkg. lasagna noodles
1 clove garlic, minced
1 lb. can of tomatoes
1 cup dry red wine
2 cans tomato paste
3 cups ricotta cheese
½ cup Parmesan cheese
1 lb. sweet sausage
1 lb. ground beef
1 tsp. salt
2 eggs
2 tbs. parsley
baking soda
1 tbs. dried basil

Cook da lasagna noodles in salted boiling water. Brown da beef and sausage ina saucepan. Skim da fat offa da top. Put in garlic, basil, salt, canned tomatoes, and tomato paste. Add da red wine. Simmer tirty minutes uncuva'd. Beat eggs wid da cheeses and da parsley.

Layer a budda'd baking dish wid noodles. Spread on halfa da cheese, den pour ova halfa da meat sauce. Make a second layer of pasta and cuva with meat and cheese. Cuva wid anudda layer of noodles. Pour sauce ova da top. Bake at 375°F until done, about tirty minutes.

DA CUVA UP

The cement overcoat is one of the mob's better known ways of disposing of stiffs to cover up their crimes. New York's East River provided the ideal location for dumping bodies weighted down with cement. Capo Anthony Strollo, a.k.a. Tony Bender, grew up in the shadow of the Manhattan Bridge; his final resting place is a bit more secure. It is speculated that Tony Bender was murdered and disposed of in the foundation of a Manhattan skyscraper.

4 tbs. olive oil
2 onions, chopped
2 cloves garlic
1 can peeled plum tomatoes
½ tsp. salt
½ tsp. oregano
¼ cup sugar
baking soda

Sauté da onions and da garlic in olive oil. Add da rest of da stuff and simmer for tirty minutes.

DA CUVA UP II

In the 1960s, ambitious, pint-sized Anthony "Tony the Ant" Spilotro got in over his head as an enforcer for the Chicago Outfit in Las Vegas. He and Frank "Lefty" Rosenthal embezzled profits from mob-owned casinos. Spilotro had a side business: his crew busted into jewelry stores to steal loot. The Chicago Outfit didn't like their boy moonlighting so they dug a hole for Tony the Ant in a cornfield and buried him alive.

3 tbs. olive oil
1 onion, chopped
1 celery stalk, diced
1 carrot, diced
½ zucchini, sliced
½ cup mushrooms
½ lb. ground beef
½ lb. sweet sausage
1 can whole peeled tomatoes
1 tbs. flour
½ cup red wine
2 cans tomato sauce
1 tsp. salt
½ tsp. marjoram
½ tsp. thyme
12 tsp. sugar
1 bay leaf

Youse sauté da vegetables in oil. In anudda pan, youse brown da beef and sausage, breaking up da sausage as youse cook. Skim off da excess fat. Trow in da flour and mix togedda well. Add wine and cook five minutes. Put da heat on a pot wid da tomatoes and sauce. Add da seasonings. Trow da meat and vegetables inta da pot wid da sauce and cook cuva'd for tirty minutes.

Part 4

SLEEPING WID DA FISHES

LOBSTER LUCCHESE

Tommy "Three-Finger Brown" Lucchese was one of New York City's original mob chieftains. Three-Finger Brown got his claws clipped in his juvenile crime days, leaving him with only seven digits. But he never lost his appetite for finger food.

2 lobsters	**1 cup butter**
2 tbs. Parmesan cheese	**1 tsp. onion, grated**
½ cup seasoned breadcrumbs	

Break da lobsters in two and crack da claws. Lay 'em meat side up unda da broiler and brush wid melted budda. Broil for 10 minutes about 4 inches from da heat. Baste frequently. Combine da breadcrumbs, cheese, and onion togedda. Sprinkle mix ova da top of da lobster. Pour melted budda ova da lobster and broil for five more minutes.

SQUID ROW

This is the final stop for many small-fry wise guys who survive the street wars and avoid jail.

3 lbs. squid | **½ cup flour**
salt | **lemon**
marinara sauce (see da cuva up, page 40)

Cut da tentacles offa tree pounds a squid and fuggedabout 'em. Dump da flour ina plastic bag. Trow da squid in and shake violently to coat. Fry da squid ina deep fryer set on 375°F until golden brown and drain on a paper towel. Serve wid dismembered lemon and marinara sauce.

GOON SQUIDS

Harry "Pittsburgh Phil" Strauss was just one of the many goons of Murder, Inc.'s death squad. Pittsburgh Phil boasted of having carried out 500 contracts. Evelyn Mittlemann was the top shooter on the women's auxiliary corps of the squad.

1½ lbs. squid, cleaned
6 tbs. parsley
¾ tsp. salt
¼ cup + 3 tbs. olive oil
1 celery root, julienne
2 heads chicory
½ tsp. pepper
3 cloves garlic
2 tbs. wine vinegar
2 tbs. lemon juice
2 cups peas
2 cups boiling water

Youse chop da tentacles offa da squid and trow 'em away. Carve da squid inta two. Slash da body of each and peel open. Put da drop on da squid ina pot of boiling water for tree minutes, until tender. Let chill. Crush da garlic and trow it ina bowl wid tree tablespoons of olive oil, 2 tablespoons of lemon juice, some parsley, da salt, and da pepper. Toss it around wid da squid; den put it on ice for tree hours.

Combine da celery root wid ¼ cup of olive oil, vinegar, and salt and pepper to taste. Rip da chicory apart and divy it up inta eight portions, den dump a scoop of da celery root in da middle. Cook da peas and toss wid da squid. Mound dis onta da celery root. Sprinkle wid parsley.

SQUID PRO QUO

Mafia recipe for staying out of jail: Mix a handful of screws with one singing canary. Throw three counts of racketeering at one greaseball. Strain greaseball with four high-priced lawyers. Add some quid pro quo and sift through the laws until the charges evaporate.

12 squid
1 clove garlic
4 anchovy fillets
3 sprigs parsley
1 lemon
2 eggs
3 tbs. breadcrumbs
olive oil
salt and pepper

Cut da tentacles offa da squid and chop 'em up wid da garlic cloves, anchovies, and parsley. Beat da eggs togedda wid da salt and pepper, and a trickle of olive oil to form a paste.

Slash open da squid and stuff da paste inside. Stab da squid wid toothpicks to close da opening. Brush wid oil, season wid salt and pepper, and broil unda moderate heat for 15 minutes. Baste wid oil da whole time. Serve wid dismembered lemon.

MORETTI'S MARINATED MUSSELS

Boss Willie Moretti wasn't the kind of thug to turn into a songbird. Moretti ran New Jersey from 1933 through the 1950s. Legend has it that Moretti was the guy that discovered Frank Sinatra. Syphilis had marinated Moretti's brain and the hit on the daffy don by Anastasia's henchmen at Joe's Restaurant in Cliffside Park, New Jersey, was considered a mercy killing.

3 lbs. mussels
3 lemons
6 basil leaves
1 clove garlic, minced
3 bell peppers
3 artichokes
½ cup olive oil
salt and pepper

Put da squeeze on a lemon ova da pot wid a quart a water. Trim da 'chokes and drown 'em in da water. Steam 'em cuva'd 'til tender. Oust da 'chokes and turn tail on a towel ta drain. Pluck da leaves off, scrap da fuzz, and cut up da bottom inta strips. Den, scorch da bell peppers, peel 'em, and cut 'em inta strips.

Scrub, scrape, and debeard da mussels and trow 'em ina pot wid halfa cuppa water and boil. Pry da shells open, pull da mussels from da shells, and trow 'em ina bowl wid da artichoke and bell pepper strips. Put da squeeze on two lemons, den add oil, garlic, salt, and pepper ova da mussels. Add thin strips of basil leaves. Marinate for four hours. Serve chilled.

MUSSEL IN

The mob muscled in on the movie industry, through their control of the unions, in the largest extortion case in U.S. history. A gang of Chicago Outfit and New York thugs, including Paul "the Waiter" Ricca, Willie Bioff, and Louis "Little New York" Campagna, extorted millions from the movie moguls by threatening strikes. Studios paid off the mob bagmen until a tip from then Screen Actors Guild president Montgomery Clift got the feds looking into the syndicate, but the goodfellas' political clout got them off.

24 mussels, cleaned
1 tbs. butter
3 tbs. parsley
4 cups dry white wine
linguini noodles, cooked
1 clove garlic
4 lbs. shrimp
2 tbs. olive oil
2 dashes Tabasco

Heat da oil and dump da mussels in. Put a lid on it and cook ova medium heat for four minutes. When da mussels open up, rip da meat outta da shells. Strain da pan juices ova da meat. Den, heat up da budda wid garlic and Tabasco, until da garlic browns. Trow in shrimp and parsley. Take da heat off when da shrimp is pink. Discharge da wine. Cook on low for two minutes. Combine da mussels and shrimp. Pour ova some linguini noodles.

CLAM UP

The slimy hands of Carlo Gambino's seasoned crumbs tried to put the squeeze on the frozen clam industry. The Gambino clan bullied buyers to force sales of the Neptune's Nuggets brand. When investigators tried to break the case, the buyers clammed up.

24 cherrystone clams
1 lb. flaked crabmeat
1 stick butter
1 onion, minced
4 lbs. mushrooms, minced
½ cup dry white wine
½ cup breadcrumbs
¼ cup fresh parsley
paprika
salt and pepper

Dunk da clams ina pot of cold water 'til dey spit out all da sand. Den youse steam da clams until da shells open. Pull da meat out and mince it.

Melt da budda ina medium saucepan. Sauté da minced onion 'til tender. Add da mushrooms and cook for four minutes. Stir in da wine, crabmeat, clams, breadcrumbs, and parsley. Season wid salt and pepper. Put crumby stuff in da shells and sprinkle paprika ova each one. Bake in da oven at 375°F for 12 minutes.

GET STEAMED

High society's favorite gangster, Joey Gallo, was whacked at Umberto's Clam House, located at the corner of Hester and Mulberry Streets in Little Italy. "Crazy Joe" got a lot of the wrong people steamed. His last meal consisted of salad, shrimp, scungilli, and clams. During a 4 a.m. dinner with his wife and sister, after having celebrated his 43rd birthday at the Copacabana nightclub on April 7, 1972, Gallo was taken out by Carmine "Sonny Pinto" DiBiase. Joey's sister, Carmella, threatened, "The streets are going to run red with blood."

12 littleneck clams
4 sticks butter
lemon wedges

Drown da clams in cold salted water for tirty minutes. Drain and repeat until dey spit out all da dirt. Trow da clams ina sauté pan and cuva dem wid water. Put a lid on it 'til da clams get steamed and open up. Melt da budda. Serve da clams steaming hot wid drawn budda and lemon wedges. Serve wid pinto soup for starters and da Gallo wine, of course.

SHARK BITES

"[T]he shark has pretty teeth, dear,
And he shows them pearly white ..."
from "Mack the Knife"

John Gotti was famous both for flashing his pearly whites and for showing his bite. As boss of the nation's most powerful Mafia sect—the Gambino family—Gotti was a hoodlum's hoodlum. The Dapper Don liked to get his hands dirty and often meted out physical punishment himself even though protocol dictated that a soldier do the job.

1 lb. shark steak **1 cup buttermilk**
1 pkg. seafood coating mix **3 cups peanut oil**
marinara sauce (see da cuva up, page 40)

Youse cut da shark up inta bite-size pieces. Dunk 'em in da buddamilk for tirty minutes. Roll 'em in seafood coating mix and shake off da excess. Trow da bites in da deep fry wid da oil heated to 375°F. Let 'em fry for two minutes. Serve wid marinara sauce.

LAND SHARK

The loan shark racket is a great source of income for the mob. Loan sharks lend money at high interest rates. When the borrower requests more funding, the loan shark deducts what is still owed and charges interest on the full amount. The consequence of non-payment is a broken leg or lost thumb.

1 lb. shark steak
1 onion, sliced
2 tbs. lemon juice
1 bay leaf
6 peppercorns
4 cups water
dash of salt
lemon wedges

Trow da onion, bay leaf, lemon juice, salt, and peppercorns ina pot of water. Put a lid on it and boil for tree minutes. Not for nuthin', add da shark and simmer for ten minutes. Serve wid lemon wedges.

SOLO BONANNO

"Joe Bananas" Bonanno, a founding Godfather of New York's original five crime families, liked to play it solo. In 1964, a Mafia commission voted to oust him from power. It is rumored that Bonanno cooked up his own kidnapping in order to prevent this from happening. Joe provoked the Banana War when he tried to make his son Bill consigliore of the family. The mob tried to ice Bonanno with bombs on three occasions. He was suspended from the commission, declared "persona non grata," and exiled to Arizona, where he lived to a ripe old age of 97, dying of natural causes in 2002.

2 lbs. sole fillets
2 tbs. clarified butter
2 bananas
1 oz. crème de banane
1 cup breadcrumbs
⅔ cup Parmesan cheese
½ cup almonds
lemon

Youse cut up da sole fillets inta bullet-size pieces. Dredge da pieces inta da mixture of breadcrumbs and Parmesan cheese to coat. Sauté da sole in budda until golden brown. Oust da sole from da pan and drain on paper towels.

Slice up da bananas and trow 'em inta da fishy budda. Add da almonds and sauté for two minutes. Dump in da banana liqueur and put da squeeze on a lemon ova da pan. Serve ova rice or pasta, spooning sauce ova da fish.

"BIG TUNA" HELPER

Tony Accardo, alias the "Big Tuna," began his criminal career as one of Al Capone's torpedoes. Accardo was the boss of the Chicago syndicate from 1943 to 1956. The Big Tuna is believed to have been a gunman at the St. Valentine's Day Massacre.

10 ripe tomatoes
1 onion, chopped
¾ cup water
1 tbs. olive oil
1 celery stalk, chopped
2 tbs. parsley
1 tsp. sugar
2 tbs. butter
2 cans tuna
1 tsp. basil
2 cloves garlic, chopped
baking soda

Youse skin and dice up da tomatoes. Put da heat on da budda and trow in da tomatoes, onion, celery, sugar, and water. Bring to a boil. Den simmer uncuva'd for 15 minutes. Trow in da seasoning and a pinch of baking soda. Simmer tirty more minutes, until da sauce thickens. Dump in da tuna, oil, and all. Keep da heat on for 10 minutes longer. Serve ova youse favorite pasta.

FRANK'S FLOUNDER

Frank Costello floundered as "Prime Minister of Organized Crime" when hard-liner mafiosi like Vito Genovese began to fear that Frankie had visions of taking over the family business. Vincent "the Chin" Gigante botched the contract. The bullet just grazed Costello's cheek even though it was fired at point-blank range. Costello was one hood who could take a hint. He retired and was the first major mobster known to have turned his back on the business and survived.

2 lbs. flounder fillets
1 cup dry white wine
2 onions
1 bell pepper
4 tbs. butter
¾ tsp. chervil
¼ tsp. salt
black pepper

Melt da budda in a large skillet. Cut da bell pepper and onions inta rings and trow 'em inta da skillet. Cook 'til da onions are transparent. Stir in da wine and seasoning. Lay da flounder in a greasy baking dish and dump da onion stuff ova it. Bake it for tirty minutes in a 350°F oven. Baste frequently.

JELLY'S FISH

One sunny afternoon, Joseph "Joey Yak" Yacovelli invited Joseph "Joe Jelly" Giorelli to go fishing. Something smelt fishy when Joe Jelly didn't return to shore. All that did come back was his overcoat wrapped around a dead fish. It was speculated that Joe Jelly ended up as crab food at the bottom of the bay.

1 lb. mackerel
2 tbs. butter
1 onion, chopped
4 oz. mushrooms, chopped
1 tbs. parsley flakes
1 tsp. fennel, crushed
½ cup breadcrumbs
½ tsp. salt

Youse melt da budda ova medium heat. Sauté da onion, mushrooms, parsley flakes, and fennel 'til da onion is see-trew. Trow in da breadcrumbs and salt. Take da heat off. Slit open da mackerel and stuff da crumb mixture inta da pocket, den close wid toothpicks. Bake ina shallow pan at 350°F for 20 minutes.

RICO FRY

The RICO statute provided prosecutors with a useful tool for convicting "connected" criminals. The crook is forced to give up all "ill-gotten" gain and serve up to 20 years in prison.

12 raw clams
1 cup flour
½ tsp. salt
1 lb. fish fillets
¾ cup warm water
12 shrimp, cleaned
3 tbs. salad oil
peanut oil
1 egg white
tartar sauce

Youse mix up da flour and salt wid da salad oil. Trow in da water and stir to blend. Let da batter rest for two hours. Beat da egg white stiff and fold it inta da batter. Cut da fish inta bullet-size pieces and dip inta da batter. Drop da fish in da deep fry of hot peanut oil set on 375°F. Pull 'em from da oil when da fish are brown. Repeat wid da shrimp and da clams. Serve wid tartar sauce.

JIMMY RIDDLE HOFFA FISH CHOWDER

President of the International Brotherhood of Teamsters from 1955 to 1967, Jimmy Hoffa had long been a "prawn" for organized crime. Jimmy could be a real chowder head. Eventually, he got himself into a stew with his mobster cronies and disappeared. It is alleged that Hoffa's final resting ground is the end zone at Giants Stadium.

½ lb. white fish, cubed
1 cup shrimp
½ cup lobster meat
8 ripe tomatoes
1 cup white wine
2 tbs. tomato paste
1 onion, diced
2 cloves garlic
½ cup crabmeat
1 lb. smoked cod fillets
6 anchovy fillets
2 tbs. olive oil
½ tsp. sugar
5 tbs. parsley
1 celery stalk
salt and pepper

Youse chop up da garlic and celery. Skin and dice da tomatoes. In a large skillet, sauté da garlic in oil. Unite togedda wid da tomatoes, da tomato paste, parsley, onion, celery, wine, and sugar wid half a cuppa water. Add a pinch a salt and pepper. Boil. Cuva and simmer for 15 minutes. Add white fish to da sauce and cook five minutes. Trow in da rest of da seafood. Simmer for tree more minutes.

Part 5

MAFIA MEAT MARKET

DA STRAIGHT BEEF

Constantino Paul Castellano had a thing for beef. His papa was a meat cutter. Big Paul's own successful meat racketeering business force fed union-controlled Manhattan supermarkets his Blue Ribbon Meats brand. Carlo Gambino appointed the meat maven head of the Cosa Nostra in 1985. Soon after, John Gotti had Castellano and his driver, Thomas Bilotti, sauced outside of Sparks Steak House on East 46th Street.

4 New York strip steaks
2½ tbs. olive oil
1½ tbs. parsley
1 tbs. sugar
12 tomatoes
2 cloves garlic
½ tsp. oregano
salt and pepper

Youse grill or pan sear da steaks to desired doneness. Skin and chop up da tomatoes. Trow 'em inta a skillet wid da udda ingredients. Bring to a boil and reduce heat. Simmer for 15 minutes. Pour da sauce ova da beef and serve.

BULL'S SLIP OF THE TONGUE

Knowledge of the Mafia has come from its members. These tongue-wagging stoolies tell their stories in order to save their own skins. Without an informer's testimony, prosecutors rarely get convictions. Salvatore "Sammy the Bull" Gravano, a beautician turned hitman, admitted to 19 murders. He is the turncoat who fingered former goombah John Gotti. Gravano served only five years for his slayings and entered the Witness Protection Program under the name Jimmy Moran.

In 2001, Sammy the Bull, along with his 23-year-old son and 27-year-old daughter, were arrested in Arizona for drug trafficking.

1 large beef tongue
1 small onion, chopped
½ cup mushrooms, chopped
1 celery stalk, chopped
1 carrot, diced
1 tbs. currants
2 tbs. wine vinegar
1 bay leaf
dash Worcestershire sauce
salt and pepper

Simmer da tongue wid everyting. Add half a cuppa water and simmer for one hour, until tongue stops wagging. When da tip of da tongue is tender, clip it off, and skin it. Trow away da bay leaf. Den, toss da vegetables inta a blender and purée wid a pinch of salt and pepper. Drown da tongue in da vegetable purée and serve.

LITTLE VEAL PISANO

Former Capone paesan and captain in the Genovese Cosa Nostra, Anthony Carfano, alias "Little Augie Pisano," organized the Butchers' Union. Little Augie Pisano must have rubbed someone the wrong way because he and his babe, dancer Janice Drake, were shot in the head on their drive home from the Gian Marino Restaurant on Lexington Avenue.

4 veal cutlets
2 eggs
2 cups flour
4 tbs. butter
½ cup dry white wine
1 lemon

Youse prepare one cutlet per person, unless Fat Tony is joining you. In that case, double da amount. Whack da cutlets 'til paper thin—pistol handles work nicely. Beat da egg and dredge da cutlets in it. Sack each cutlet wid flour and shake 'em down. Put da heat on da budda in a large skillet and brown da cutlets. Bounce da veal from da pan and trow in da wine. Put da squeeze on da lemon ova da pan and stir. Add fuel to da fire until boiling. Take da heat off and return cutlets to da pan. Cook ova low heat for 10 minutes. Serve wid da pan sauce.

GREASEBALLS

La Cosa Nostra was steeped in mystery until a greaseball named Joseph Valachi blew the lid off the secret society in the 1960s. Valachi, a soldier in the Genovese crime family, described the inner workings of the Mafia in great detail to the feds and to television audiences watching the Senate hearings. While Valachi's testimony never led to any arrests, he did help identify over 300 made guys and coached his guards in the art of making meatballs.

1 lb. ground beef
2 eggs
½ cup seasoned breadcrumbs
1 tsp. grated lemon rind
1 tsp. granulated garlic
3 tbs. parsley
2 tbs. Parmesan cheese
1 tbs. olive oil
salt and pepper
¼ tsp. oregano

Punch a hole in da ground beef and trow da eggs and seasonings in it. Mix it good wid youse two hands. Grease youse palms wid oil and roll da beef inta little golf ball-size meatballs. Brown ina skillet wid hot oil 'til done.

ANASTASIA'S BEEF

Albert "Mad Hatter" Anastasia, Lord High Executioner of Murder, Inc., was always beefed about something. When the Mad Hatter heard about the capture of the notorious bank robber, Willie Sutton, he was beefed at the guy who fingered Sutton and ordered a hit on the stool pigeon—even though he didn't know either man. Anastasia was later cut down at the barber shop of the Park Sheraton Hotel in 1957. The hit parade was led by the three Gallo brothers.

2 lbs. ground beef
1 onion, chopped
2 cans tomato sauce
1 bell pepper, sliced
mozzarella cheese
2 eggplants
1 tsp. salt
½ tsp. oregano
½ tsp. basil
black pepper

Brown da beef ina little hot oil. Cook for two minutes wid da onion and bell pepper. Add tomato sauce and seasonings. Keep it stirred for 10 minutes ova medium heat. Cut da eggplants inta slices and lay 'em out ina shallow baking dish. Smother da eggplant wid da sauce and bake at 350°F for 20 minutes. Top wid mozzarella cheese and bake until da cheese is melted.

THE FAST BUCK

Young gang members get hooked on crime as a means to a fast buck. Murder was the membership requirement for wannabe Whyos—one of New York's legendary gangs. The Whyos marketed their skills by posting a price list:

Punching	*$2*
Chewing Off Ear	*$15*
Giving Two Black Eyes	*$4*
Stabbing or Shooting	*$25*
Breaking Nose & Jaw	*$10*
"Doing the Job"	*$100*

4 lbs. venison roast
½ cup red wine
1 celery stalk, chopped
1 small onion, chopped
bacon strips
2 whole cloves
1 bay leaf
1 lemon
½ lb. beef suet
salt and pepper

Lay da roast to rest ina deep pan. Dump da wine ova da meat. Put in da onion and celery. Squeeze da lemon ova it all. Add da cloves and beef suet. Salt and pepper to taste. Put a lid on it and simmer until tender ina 350°F oven for tirty minutes. Cover da roast wid bacon strips and broil 'til da bacon crisps.

MOMO SAUSAGE

Salvatore "Momo" Giancana, a.k.a. "Sam Mooney," got his piece of the pie when he was boss of the Chicago Outfit. Sam shared a mistress with President Kennedy. He ruled his Mafia family with an iron hand, but he was unable to control his Mafia Princess daughter. In 1975, Momo was cooking sausages in his Oak Park, Illinois, home when he was plugged with a bullet to the back of the head and six in the mouth.

1 lb. sweet Italian sausage
3 cups red wine
salt and pepper
3 green peppers
3 tsp. olive oil

Carve da stems and seeds outta da peppers and chop 'em up inta large chunks. Sauté da peppers in olive oil until soft. Sprinkle dem wid a little salt and pepper. Cut sausages in pieces. Brown da sausages in an oven-proof skillet. Den dump da wine in, cuva da pan, and bake at 350°F for 40 minutes. Put da peppers in and bake for anudda tirty minutes.

ROAST SQUEALER

The mob often bids out its dirty work. Cecil Kirby, a Canadian biker, was one punk who earned his keep as a contract killer. He also sold drugs and provided other sundry services. Kirby became a contract squealer for the feds when he heard the mob had bid out a contract on him.

4 lbs. pork loin	**5 tbs. water**
6 cloves garlic	**5 tbs. red wine**
1 tsp. rosemary	**salt and pepper**

Scar da squealer wid a knife across its skin. Stab da flesh of each a da joints and stuff one garlic clove and da rosemary inta each. Press anudda four cloves of garlic inta da meat. Trow da pig inta a roasting pan and pour water and wine ova it. Season wid salt and pepper. Cook at 350°F for 2 hours. Not for nuttin', baste it once ina while.

ON THE LAM

Whether the heat is on from the cops or the mob is busting your chops, when ewe have a baad yen to get away from it all, every dyed-in-the-wool mafioso has a safe place to go on the lam.

12 baby lamb chops
1 cup olive oil
3 sprigs sage
½ cup dry white wine
1 lemon
salt and pepper

Turn da heat up on da olive oil ina medium skillet. Add tree sprigs of sage. Trow da chops in and brown on both sides. Season wid salt and pepper. Dump da wine in and simmer until da chops are real tender. Put da squeeze on da lemon. Serve right away.

WEISS-GUY SURPRISE

Prohibition gangster Earl "Hymie" Weiss was said to have invented the term "one-way ride." This method would involve luring the victim into the passenger seat of the car. A trigger-man in the backseat zotzes the sucker and the stiff is pushed out the door at a suitably desolate destination as the car speeds away.

The first person to meet his maker in this fashion was Steve Wisniewski in 1921. Wisniewski had evidently hijacked the wrong beer truck.

4 veal cutlets
2 cups flour
5 eggs
2 tsp. milk
2 cups seasoned breadcrumbs
4 tbs. olive oil
4 anchovy fillets
lemon wedges

Beat da cutlets to a pulp. Coat da veal wid flour, den shake off da excess. Pistol-whip da eggs wid da milk. Dip da veal in it. Sift da seasoned breadcrumbs and coat da cutlets. Brown da veal for 10 minutes. Cap off da cutlets wid a fried egg. Garnish wid lemon wedges and rolled anchovies.

APALACHIN BARBECUE

Joseph "Joe the Barber" Barbara, owner of a soft drink bottling plant, hosted the famed Mafia meeting at his home in Apalachin, New York. This was an attempt by the Mafia's hierarchy to calm the family rivalries that had erupted with the hit on Albert Anastasia. The state police raided the joint before anything was settled. Mobsters jumped out of windows and fled through the woods to avoid capture and notoriety.

4 lbs. spareribs
¾ cup wine vinegar
2 tbs. onion, chopped
1 tbs. light brown sugar
½ tsp. dry mustard
1 garlic clove, chopped
¼ cup Worcestershire sauce
1 onion, quartered
½ cup ketchup
1 tbs. lemon juice
¼ tsp. black pepper
¼ cup chili sauce
cayenne pepper

Youse trow togedda ina pan everyting but da ribs and onion. Simmer dis sauce for one hour, keeping it stirred. Trow da ribs in a large pan wid da quartered onion. Cuva wid water and boil. Simmer on low heat 1½ hours. Drain den grill da ribs ova low coals, brushing frequently wid da sauce.

HERO WORSHIP

Eliot Ness led federal agents in the fight against organized crime. Ness creatively used the press to make himself the most famous fed. He often notified the media before a bust in order to ensure full coverage and credit for the event.

1 loaf Italian bread
¼ lb. pastrami
¼ lb. capicolo
¼ lb. prosciutto
¼ lb. provolone cheese
1 head lettuce, shredded
2 tomatoes, sliced
black pepper
spicy hot mustard
double-dealer dressing **(see page 94)**

Cut da Italian bread wide open right down da middle and spread mustard on both sides. Lay out da meats and cheeses. Top wid lettuce and tomato. Sprinkle wid pepper. Drizzle wid double-dealer dressing, fold ova, and eat.

O'BANION'S CORNED BEEF

Dean Charles "Dion" O'Banion was the head of Chicago's Irish mob during Prohibition. Dion was absent from the SMC Cartage Company warehouse that famous Valentine's Day when his gang was rubbed out. Capone's torpedoes eventually caught up with Dion at his legitimate business—a flower shop. Once the job was done, they sent elaborate floral creations to his funeral.

1 lean brisket beef
1 head cabbage
3 anchovy fillets
3 cocktail onions
1 tsp. Dijon mustard
3 tbs. olive oil
2 tbs. wine vinegar
dash of white pepper

Cuva da brisket wid water ina large pot and boil. Trim da cabbage and boil in anudda pot. Trow togedda a sauce by mashing da anchovies and onions wid da mustard, olive oil, vinegar, and white pepper. Slice a little of da corned beef and stash da slices between da cabbage leaves. Pour da sauce ova da cabbage and serve wid da remaining corned beef.

"CHICAGO PIANO" CHILI

This rapid-fire chili is guaranteed to repeat on you like the "Tommy Gun" it is named after. The gun was invented by Brigadier General John Thompson in the 1920s and quickly became the underworld's favorite tool of terror. At $175, it was a steal for gangland shooters. Present-day hitmen prefer the Glock 17.

2 lbs. ground beef
4 cans kidney beans
1 onion, chopped
2 tbs. Worcestershire sauce
1 can tomato paste
¾ tbs. Tabasco sauce
2 cans peeled tomatoes
cayenne pepper
¼ tsp. cumin seeds
¼ lb. hot sausage
8 tbs. chili powder
1 tbs. steak sauce
1 clove garlic, chopped
½ tsp. oregano
½ cup dry red wine
cheddar cheese, grated

Youse cook da sausage and reserve da drippings. Den youse brown da beef in sausage drippings, onion, and garlic. Trow in all da udda stuff and simmer ova low heat for tree hours. Serve da chili piping hot wid grated cheddar cheese ova da top.

Part 6

DA BOIDS

FOWL PLAY

The syndicate has many ways of cooking up foul play. Some of the gamier dishes have established the pecking order of the mob. The famous clandestine meeting of organized crime's top guns was the first to set the ground rules on a national scale. The meeting was held in 1929 at the President Hotel in Atlantic City. The big boys in attendance included Frank Costello, Lucky Luciano, Meyer Lansky, Dutch Schultz, Joe Adonis, Lepke Buchalter, Johnny Torrio, Al Capone, Albert Anastasia, Greasy Thumb Guzik, Moe Dalitz, King Solomon, and Longy Zwillman.

1 medium chicken, quartered
8 ripe tomatoes
½ cup chicken stock
1 onion, chopped
5 tbs. Marsala wine
salt and pepper
4 tbs. tomato paste
2½ cups mushrooms, sliced
2 cloves garlic, chopped
4 tbs. butter
1 tsp. sugar
1¼ tbs. olive oil

Coat da boid in flour and brown ina pan wid budda and olive oil. Bounce da boid when browned and trow da onion and garlic in da pan. Skin and chop up da tomatoes and drop in da pan wid tomato paste, sugar, chicken stock, and seasoning. Boil. Trow da boid back in da pan. Simmer tirty minutes. Add da mushrooms and Marsala wine and cook 15 more minutes. Serve wid some pasta.

MURDER MOST FOWL

In 1991, warring factions were fighting for control of the Columbo organized crime family. Carmine Persico was in jail and acting boss Victor Oreno wanted to rule the clan. Oreno henchmen had a standing order to kill anyone loyal to Persico. Father and son Anthony and Christopher Liberatore were dispatched to the Wanna Bagel Shop in Bay Ridge, Brooklyn, to kill the owners who were believed to be part of the Persico faction. The owners were not in, but they followed their orders to execute anyone at hand and shot the counter boy, 17-year-old Matteo Speranza, six times. The Liberatores cut a deal with the FBI to enter the Witness Protection Program.

6 large eggs
1 red onion, chopped
2 cloves garlic, minced
1 cup milk
¼ tsp. fresh parsley
mozzarella cheese
1 small zucchini
1 sweet pepper, chopped
2 tsp. olive oil
¼ tsp dried oregano
Parmesan cheese
salt and pepper

Heat oil and sauté da zucchini, onion, garlic, and pepper until tender. Beat da eggs and milk wid oregano, parsley, salt, and pepper. Add vegetables to egg mixture and pour inta a pie pan. Bake at 350°F oven for tirty minutes. Let it stand on da counter for five minutes. Sprinkle wid mozzarella and Parmesan cheese and serve wid bagels.

"TWO-GUNS" CHICKEN

Louis "Two Gun" Alterie, a.k.a. "Kid Haynes," was no chicken. When his pal, Samuel "Nails" Morton died after being thrown off a horse, Two Guns shot the horse. A crony in Chicago's Irish mob, Louis challenged Capone's torpedoes to a shootout at sunset after the St. Valentine's Day Massacre. Fearing the shooters might actually take him up on his offer, Louis packed his pistols and moved to Colorado.

4 lbs. chicken, quartered
1 celery stalk, chopped
1 tbs. salt
2 cups mushrooms, sliced
1 tsp. black peppercorns
1 bay leaf
2 onions
2 oz. pimento, chopped
1 bell pepper, chopped
1 tsp. sugar
2 cups chicken broth
5 qts. water

Youse trow da chicken ina deep pot wid one whole onion, da peppercorns, salt, sugar, bay leaf, and celery. Drown in five quarts of water for tree hours. Bounce da chicken from da pot. Tear da meat offa da bones and chop inta tiny pieces. Strain da broth and reserve two cups. Cook pasta of your choice in remaining broth.

In da two cups of broth, sauté mushrooms, one chopped onion, bell pepper, and pimento until onion is translucent. Stir in da chicken pieces and serve ova pasta.

YOUNG TURK

The over-achievers in the Mafia have a distinct habit of giving the "kiss of death" to the outmoded ways of their bosses. A young turk's rise to power is often swift and violent. Carmine "Cigar" Galante's path to the top of the Bonanno heap was hastened by a great deal of carnage. He clipped journalist Carlo Tresca in 1943 on orders from don Vito Genovese, who had the radical reporter cut down to please Benito Mussolini. The Cigar knocked off eight top mafiosi in 1978 alone. A year later, Galante had his wings clipped in Joe and Mary's Restaurant in Brooklyn, a cigar still clenched in his teeth.

2 turkey legs
3 tbs. unsalted butter
1 cup dry white wine
1 cup chicken broth
zest of 1 lemon
4 tbs. olive oil
½ tsp. sage
1 tsp. rosemary
1 garlic clove
2 tbs. parsley

Break da boid's legs in tree and dredge in flour. Sear in olive oil wid budda 'til brown. Mash da lemon zest, rosemary, sage, and garlic wid parsley and trow it in da pan. Cook tree minutes. Add wine. When da wine evaporates, season wid salt and pepper and trow in da chicken broth. Boil. Put a lid on it, simmer, and fuggedaboudit for 25 minutes. Dump da sauce ova da broken legs and serve.

STOOL PIGEON

Abe "Kid Twist" Reles, the state's prize stool pigeon on Murder, Inc.'s dirty deeds, became the fall guy at the Half Moon Hotel on Coney Island. The pigeon mysteriously took flight out the window of a heavily guarded room, plummeting to his death. After the plunge, one million posters were issued to apprehend Murder, Inc.'s diabolical duo, Lepke Buchalter and Albert Anastasia.

4 squabs
½ cup Marsala wine
¼ lb. chicken livers
6 tbs. butter
2 cups flour
white truffle, sliced

Youse wash da boids and wipe 'em dry. Den youse dunk dem in flour and salt mixture. Drop da pigeons ina skillet of melted budda. Add wine and cook rapidly for five minutes. Dump in a half cuppa hot water and cook ova medium heat for tirty minutes. Ten minutes before da boids are ready to talk, add da chicken livers and sliced truffle. Serve up da pigeon sauced.

MONGOOSE

"Mongoose" was the code name for the joint CIA–Mafia plot to cook Fidel Castro's goose. "Big Jim" O'Connell was the CIA agent in charge of the assassination plot. Castro had put a damper on mob-controlled casino operations in Cuba, giving the syndicate a vested interest in the leader's demise.

1 goose
2 cups flour
salt and pepper
1 cup milk
½ cup salad oil

If youse can't filch a goose, get youse hands on a wild duck. Break da boid inta six pieces. Season wid salt and pepper, den dredge in flour. Sauté da goose slowly in hot salad oil for tirty minutes, turning it often. Add milk. Put a lid on it and simmer for an hour. Serve wid pan sauce ova da boid.

Part 7

SIDES & SALADS

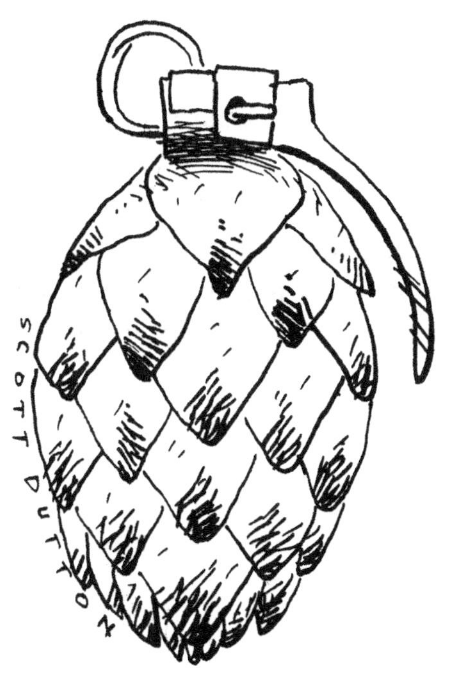

THE BRONX CHOKE

"Italians gotta have artichokes." The words of Bronx vice lord Gino Terranove inspired the mobsters to try and corner the New York artichoke market. Terranove monopolized the market to fix prices, putting a choke hold on the grocery stores and vegetable sellers.

artichokes **butter** **salt**

Youse make one artichoke for each guest. Give da bounce ta da stems and first row of leaves. Nip da tips offa da leaves. Drown da 'chokes in cold salted water for tirty minutes. Drain on a paper towel. Line 'em up ina saucepan. Trow in 4 inches of boiling water and a pinch of salt and let dem simmer for tirty minutes. Turn tail on a towel to drain. Serve wid melted budda.

CHOKES WITH BATED BREATH

To be eaten immediately prior to a police interrogation to keep the screws at a distance.

6 tbs. olive oil
1 tbs. wine vinegar
4 slices ham
1 clove garlic
2 tbs. lemon juice
4 artichokes
salt and pepper

Beat up da olive oil and lemon juice togedda wid da vinegar. Salt and pepper to taste. Trow in da garlic clove and dump it in a jar. Put a lid on it and lock it up ova night.

Pluck da hearts outta da artichokes and put da drop on 'em inta da garlic dressing. Fuggedaboudit! Marinate for as long as youse want. Chop up da sliced ham and sprinkle ova da top of da 'chokes before serving.

GARMENT DISTRICT CHOKES

Lepke Buchalter was an enterprising thug who founded Murder, Inc. His control of the garment district rackets insured Lepke a ready supply of snappy suits in case one got messed up from his work as a contract killer. Buchalter was the only top dog to take a hot squat in the electric chair for his crimes.

artichokes **oil**
lemon juice

Dese artichokes, like Lepke, are fried. Youse fix one 'choke per person, so don't nobody get greedy. Drown fully dressed artichokes in cold water wid da juice of a lemon. Fuggedaboudit for tirty minutes. Dis will break down da resistance and da 'chokes will open right up. Fill a deep fryer wid five inches of oil and turn da heat on 300°F. Grab da 'chokes by da stems wid long tongs and hold unda da hot oil. Da oil will make a lot of noise so don't go in too deep. Push da 'chokes ta da bottom and pull out when brown. Turn tail on a towel to drain and serve.

SPILL DA BEANS

Dozens of top ranking Mafia heads rolled when witness Philip Leonetti spilled the beans on his involvement in the Philadelphia-Atlantic City mob—the crime family that controlled the unions and owned the steel and concrete companies that built the casinos. Leonetti, the youngest underboss in the country and admitted killer of 10, broke omerta (the code of silence) to save his own skin. Leonetti was initiated into the Mafia at age ten, when he accompanied his uncle Nicky Scarfo to dispose of a stiff.

2 lbs. fresh green beans
3 tbs. olive oil
3 tbs. fresh oregano
4 plum tomatoes, chopped
6 cloves garlic, minced
salt and pepper

Clip da tips and snap da beans in two. Blanch in boiling water for two minutes to soften. Drain well. Ina large skillet, sauté da garlic in hot oil until soft. Put in da tomatoes, oregano, salt, and pepper. Simmer uncuva'd, until tomatoes break down. Add da green beans and cook uncuva'd 'til tender. Add seasonings as needed.

ZANY ZUC-CHINI

In 2003, zany Vincent "the Chin" Gigante admitted to feigning insanity for thirty years. He plead guilty to labor racketeering on the city's waterfront. The Chin rose to the leadership of the Genovese crime family when head honcho Anthony "Fat Tony" Salerno was sentenced to 100 years in prison in the 1987 Commission Case. The "Oddfather" faked insanity to avoid trial. His priest brother Father Louis swore to the press that his brother was a mentally ill "mama's boy" with an IQ of 70, and the Chin strolled around his Little Italy neighborhood in pajamas and a bathrobe.

6 zucchini
5 tbs. breadcrumbs
3 tbs. Parmesan, grated
6 oz. prosciutto
3 tbs. parsley, minced
3 eggs
1 tbs. butter
2 tbs. olive oil

Clip da ends offa da zucchini. Steam for five minutes 'til tender. Let dem cool off. Slit da zucchini down da middle. Scrape out da pulp. Cut da prosciutto inta strips. Beat da eggs. Trow togedda breadcrumbs, cheese, budda, and meat. Stuff da mix up inta da zucchini shells. Lay out ina baking dish, wid olive oil and two tablespoons a water. Dot wid budda and sprinkle wid cheese. Bake at 350°F for tirty minutes.

SMALL POTATOES

When they called him a nickle and dime operator, Jack "Machine Gun" McGurn wanted to show the mob that he was not small potatoes by pressing a nickle into the palm of his victims' hands. Machine Gun was a shooter in the St. Valentine's Day Massacre and bought it himself at a bowling alley on the anniversary of the bloodbath.

2 lbs. red potatoes
parsley
olive oil
salt and pepper

Cut da taters inta quarters, not nickels. Roast da spuds at 400°F for tirty minutes. Sprinkle wid oil, parsley, salt, and pepper to taste halfway trew da tirty minutes.

DA MOBSTER MASH

Mobsters have a nasty penchant for knocking one another off. In 1928, Frankie Yale, head of the notorious Black Hand, was mashed in a spray of bullets on 44th Street in Brooklyn. The hit was the first to use a submachine gun in a New York gang war. The bejeweled stiff donned a belt inset with 75 diamonds, a 3-karat diamond stick pin, and 3-karat and 4-karat diamond rings.

1 lb. potatoes
½ cup flour
1 tsp. butter
1 egg
¼ cup Parmesan cheese
salt and pepper

Don't peel da spuds. Boil dem ina large pot a water 'til tender. Drain. Take da heat off and fuggedaboudit! Tirty minutes later, pounce on da spuds 'til finely mashed. Rub out trew a sieve.

Trow da mash ina bowl wid flour and budda. Beat da egg and add to da mash. Season wid salt and pepper. Youse could add a pinch of garlic salt now. Whip until smooth.

Wid damp hands, shape da mash inta small balls. Put da drop on da balls ova a saucepan of boiling salted water. Boil da balls 'til dey can't take any more and dey float to da top. Sprinkle wid shaved budda and grated Parmesan cheese. Dat's da way youse do da mobster mash.

SWINDLER'S SALAD

The dressing has bite—and it should. A 250-pound swindler, Anthony "Tino" De Angelis, sunk his teeth into the international salad oil industry by conning Wall Street commodities houses. Allied Crude Vegetable Oil Refining Corporation looked great on paper. The company traded on enormous quantities of soybean, cottonseed, and other oils that it stored in 100 tanks in Bayonne, New Jersey. The business made Tino a big player in the government's Food for Peace Program. When Tino started trading on futures and IOUs, Wall Street didn't care as long as he was profitable. The rumors that Tino was backed by the Mafia helped. In 1964, Tino failed to meet his "margin call." By the time creditors descended to find empty oil tanks, the great salad oil swindle involved losses of $150 million.

2 heads romaine lettuce
6 cherry tomatoes, halved
2 onions, sliced
1 cup olives
2 carrots, grated

Rip da lettuce to shreds and dump ina big bowl wid da grated carrots, sliced onions, and halved tomatoes and olives. Toss violently.

DOUBLE-DEALER DRESSING

Don't go to Tino for the salad oil; the New Jersey warehouses provided to him by American Express were usually empty.

4 cups salad oil
2 cups red wine vinegar
½ cup Parmesan, grated
1 small onion, diced
1 bell pepper, diced
1 tsp. granulated garlic
2 tbs. sugar
1 tbs. pepper
1 tbs. oregano
1 tbs. salt
1 tbs. thyme
1 tbs. basil

Mix up all da ingredients ina bowl and chill for two hours. Toss salad wid dressing. Youse could add prosciutto, anchovies, salami, or make someting up to add.

UNITY DAY SALAD

Joe Colombo organized the Italian-American Civil Rights League to protest FBI harassment of Italians. The league was a front for his less colorful activities. Colombo successfully protested to have the word "Mafia" expunged from the movie The Godfather. *The mob disapproved of Colombo's headline-grabbing antics and a hit was made at the Unity Day rally at Columbus Circle on June 17, 1971. Pal Joey was rendered a vegetable by the bullet. He died seven years later and was laid to rest at his own funeral parlor in Brooklyn.*

4 lbs. fresh green beans
8 cups cannellini beans
2 cups parsley, minced
5 garlic cloves, minced
½ cup red wine vinegar
72 radishes, sliced
2 green onions, chopped
2 cups olive oil
4 ½ tsp. lemon juice

Nip da tips and break da beans in two. Boil da green beans in salted water 'til tender, den cool. Stir togedda da garlic, oil, juice, parsley, and vinegar. Toss wid da udda stuff to serve 20 people.

LITTLE CAESAR SALAD

The salad is generally reserved for the last course in an Italian meal. In the salad days of Al Capone's unsavory activities, he once clobbered three of his dinner guests with a baseball bat in a fit of rage, telling each to skip the last course.

1 garlic clove, sliced
1 egg
dash of salt
3 tbs. wine vinegar
croutons
anchovies
½ cup olive oil
2 heads romaine lettuce
1 lemon
dash of dry mustard
Parmesan cheese, grated

Drown da garlic ova night in olive oil. Reserve da oil and discard da garlic. Rip up da lettuce and trow ina bowl wid da udda seasonings. Douse wid da oil and vinegar. Put da drop on da egg and da squeeze on da lemon. Toss gently. Top off wid croutons, anchovies, and grated Parmesan cheese.

"MAD DOG" COLL-SLAW

Vincent "Mad Dog" Coll was an ambitious young thug from Irish mob Hell's Kitchen. He hooked up with the mob as an enforcer for Dutch Schultz. Coll aspired to have his own gang and tried to coax the Dutchman's top gun, Vinnie Barelli, to join him. When Barelli declined his offer, Mad Dog slaughtered him and his babe in cold blood. In 1932, Schultz's torpedoes caught up with Coll at a drugstore phone booth on West 23rd Street. Fifteen bullets stilled the 23 year old's aspirations forever.

1 large cabbage
1 cup sugar
1 onion, sliced
⅔ cup salad oil
1 tbs. celery salt
1 tbs. dry mustard
1 cup wine vinegar

Rip da cabbage to shreds and sprinkle wid da sugar. Add da onion and toss. Ina saucepan, trow togedda da rest of da ingredients. Bring to a boil and keep stirred. Pour da hot sauce ova da cabbage and toss. Put it on ice. Serve in eight hours.

SALLY'S FRUIT SALAD

Salvatore "Sally" De Vita was a transvestite hood whose specialty was hijacking. Sally attempted to perfect the art of woman's dress and makeup, yet always managed to look like a big Mafia hood in drag. His favorite heists were designer dresses and he invariably carried a pistol underneath the filched frock.

2 cans mandarin oranges
6 bananas, sliced
1 can crushed pineapples
1 bag mini marshmallows
2 eggs, beaten
1 cup sugar
1 tbs. flour
1 pkg. peach Jell-O

Mix up da drained pineapple juice, eggs, sugar, and flour. Put ova low heat for tree minutes. Add Jell-O mix. Stir it up. Cool it off and add fruit and marshmallows. Refrigerate and fuggedaboudit for tree hours.

Part 8

SWEET ENDINGS

MAFIA-STYLE CHEESECAKE

Wise guys are always surrounded by plenty of cheesecake. Called main squeeze, gangster's moll, and barracuda, many famous broads were attracted by the romantic notions of organized crime. Goodfellas take their wives out on Friday night and keep the rest of the week for their mistresses. Sam Giancana had a long friendship with Phyllis McGuire of the singing McGuire Sisters and Longy Zwillman financed Jean Harlow's acting career.

⅔ cup soft butter
1 lemon peel, grated
2 tbs. + 1 cup flour
2 tbs. milk
8 oz. cream cheese
3 egg yolks
3 tbs. + 1 cup sugar
3 eggs

Beat togedda da budda, a cuppa flour, tree tablespoons a sugar, an egg yolk, and halfa da lemon peel. Roll it inta a ball and put on ice for an hour. Press a third of da dough onta da bottom of a 10 inch by 3 inch springform pan. Bake it at 400°F for eight minutes. Cool it!

Beat da cream cheese 'til smooth wid a mixer on low speed. Trow in a cuppa sugar and da rest of da ingredients. Turn mixer up to medium and beat for five minutes. Press da remaining dough around da sides of da springform pan. Pour da cheese in and bake 10 minutes at 375°F. Turn oven to 300°F and bake 20 more minutes. Chill and serve.

SWEETHEART DEAL

The federal Witness Protection Program is a sweetheart deal. Most made guys have difficulty staying on the straight and narrow once in the program. Of those that took the deal, more than 37 are back in prison. Even wise guy Henry Hill has been convicted of burglary, assault, and drunk driving since entering the program.

1 can condensed milk
⅔ cup coconut macaroons
2 tsp. vanilla extract
½ cup maraschino cherries
3 egg yolks
½ cup light rum
½ cup almonds
2 cups cream

Beat da tree egg yolks hard. Trow 'em ina large bowl wid everyting except da cream. Mix it all up.

Pistol-whip da cream to light and fluffy. Fold da whipped cream inta da egg mixture. Pour da stuff inta foil cups and cuva. Put 'em in da deep freeze for six hours. Makes about two dozen.

ILL-GOTTEN GAIN

Maier Suchowljansky, better known as Meyer Lansky, was the syndicate's most durable felon. His calculating mind organized the mob's money laundering operations and quietly set up gambling cartels in the Bahamas, Cuba, Haiti, and South America. He often bragged that the mob was bigger than U.S. Steel. A thrifty hood, his holdings at the time of his death in 1983 were estimated at $300 million.

6 egg yolks
4 tbs. sugar
½ cup Marsala wine
whipped cream
shaved chocolate
4 sugar cookies

Trow da yolks and sugar in a double-boiler. Whack it 'til it's creamy, slowly beating in da wine. Set da pot ova simmering water in da bottom of da boiler. Continue ta beat da stuff 'til it thickens. It should take about tree minutes. Don't overheat. Take da heat off. Dump da zabaglione inta sherbet dishes and top wid whipped cream and shaved chocolate. Serve wid cookies.

G-MEN COOKIES

J. Edgar Hoover was director of the FBI from 1924–1972. Hoover did not believe there was a Mafia until he heard Joe Valachi's revelations during the Kefauver hearings, also known as the Special Committee on Organized Crime in Interstate Commerce. "Government men," called "G-Men" by mobsters, became Hoover's chief weapon against organized crime in the U.S.

½ cup confectioners' sugar
3 tbs. candied ginger
¼ tsp. ground dried ginger
1 tsp. vanilla extract
½ lb. butter
2 tbs. flour
¼ cup cornstarch

Wise guys like ta eat da G-Men cookies head first. Cream da budda wid sugar and vanilla. Beat it hard for tree minutes. Sift togedda flour and cornstarch. Trow in da ginger, both kinds. Split da dough in two. Roll out da dough and shape to resemble a G-Man. Prick da head wid an ice pick. Put 'em on ice for tirty minutes. Sprinkle a baking sheet wid confectioners' sugar and line up da G-Men on a baking sheet. Bake at 325°F for 25 minutes.

ONE TOUGH COOKIE

Virginia Hill was one tough cookie who taunted and teased federal investigators, but gave no information about the gangsters she was intimate with. Hill decorated the Las Vegas Flamingo Casino during her tenure as mistress to Bugsy Siegel. Prior to falling hard for Siegel, Hill was mistress to many of the big boys of the day. The list included Joe Adonis, Frank Costello, Tony Accardo, Frank Nitti, and the Fishetti brothers.

2½ cups flour
1 tsp. baking powder
1 tsp. cinnamon
1 tsp. vanilla
1 cup butter
3 egg yolks
1 cup sugar
pinch of salt

Cream da budda wid sugar, beating 'til fluffy. Trow in da tree yolks one atta time. Continue to beat. Stir up wid everyting else. Shape a heaping spoonful of dough inta a 2½-inch long cookie. Roll each cookie in sesame seeds. Put 'em on a baking sheet and bake at 400°F for eight minutes to make five dozen.

KISS OF DEATH

The movie Kiss of Death, *starring Richard Widmark as gangster Tommy Udo, had a big impact on a young mob wannabe named John Gotti, who saw the movie six times and adopted Udo's maniacal "he-he-he" laugh and swagger as his own.*

3 cups dried chestnuts
½ tsp. vanilla essence
¼ pt. heavy cream
1 tbs. milk
pinch of salt
¾ cup superfine sugar
2 tbs. rum
confectioners' sugar
2 tbs. chocolate, grated

Soak da chestnuts ova night. Drain. Trow in da pan and cuva wid cold water. Boil, cuva, and simmer about tirty minutes. Drain and mash wid a fork.

Stir in da sugar, vanilla, a pinch a salt, and half da rum. Press trew a sieve and let it fall ina mound inta a small bowl. Beat up da cream and milk togedda 'til stiff. Stir in da rest of da rum and add a little confectioners' sugar to taste. Spoon ova da chestnut stuff. Den sprinkle wid chocolate. Serve straight away.

Part 9

DUTCH'S HOME BREW

Arthur Flegenheimer's fast rise to becoming the "beer baron" of Prohibition made him one of gangland's most notorious characters. He came to regret changing his name to Dutch Shultz, a name that fit so neatly into headlines when he was tagged public enemy number one. It was that name recognition that caused Lucky Luciano to give the order to suds the Dutchman. His last stop for refreshments was the Palace Chophouse in Newark, New Jersey.

1 pkg. active dry yeast
1 can Blue Ribbon malt
4 lbs. sugar
30 qts. water

Youse fill a 40-quart barrel wid halfa da water. Mix da malt togedda wid an equal amount of water. Dissolve da yeast in warm water. Trow da malt in da barrel wid da yeast and sugar and stir it up. Add anudda 15 quarts of water ta da barrel. Fuggedaboudit for six days. Bottle da beer when bubbles rise to da top. Beer should stand for a week before drinking. For da best taste, let it alone for six months, den drink it. It yields 33 quarts at 12 percent alcohol.

Part 10

TERMS YOUSE CAN'T LIVE WIDOUT

Batter Sometin dat can be beaten.

Clarify Clear it up by adding a beaten egg white and egg shell. Da egg coagulates in hot liquid and da liquid is den strained.

Coddle Cook up slowly and gently just below boiling point.

Cream Beat it 'til it goes soft.

Cube Cut in even pieces.

Cut Divide wid a knife.

Dice Cut up inta smaller cubes.

Dismember Cut up and pull apart.

Dissolve To pass inta solution.

Fold Combine, beginning wid a downward motion across da bottom of da bowl and ending wid an up and ova motion.

Grate	Run ova a grater ta shred inta tiny unidentifiable particles.
Juice	Da pay-off when youse put da squeeze on it.
Knead	Ta press dough wid youse knuckles and fold it repeatedly.
Marinate	Leave stuff in liquid ta make it tender.
Mince	Ta cut food inta very fine pieces.
Pare	Shave outer skin wid a sharp object.
Peel	Ta strip off outer skin wid youse bare hands.
Pistol-Whip	Beat violently in a circular motion.
Da Squeeze On	Ta squeeze da juice out of it.
Scald	Heat 'til it blisters forming tiny bubbles at da edge of da pot.
Shred	Tear up inta very tin slices.
Simmer	Ta cook in liquid just below da boiling point. Bubbles form and collapse below da surface.
Skim	Ta remove da scum offa da top.
Slice	Your portion of da stuff.
Zotze	Ta thoroughly cook ta kill all bacteria.

Part 11

SUSPICIOUS STAINS

Blood Pre-soak in cold water for tirty minutes. If stain remains, soak in ammonia water (3 tablespoons ammonia per gallon of water). Rinse.

Candle Wax Use a dull blade ta scrape wax off and place tissues ova da fabric and press wid a warm iron.

Grass Pre-soak in cold water for tirty minutes. Rinse and pre-treat wid detergent and hot water. Or, use one part alcohol to two parts water.

Grease/Tar Rub spot wid lard and sponge wid dry cleaning solvent. Wash in hot water and detergent.

Liquor Rinse wid white vinegar, den cold water.

Lipstick Loosen stain wid non-flammable dry cleaning solvent. Rub detergent in 'til da stain outline is gone. Wash in hot water.

Scorch Wash wid detergent and bleach. Or, cuva da stain wid a cloth dampened in hydrogen peroxide. Cuva dis wid dry cloth and press wid hot iron. Rinse well.

Wine Rub wid concentrated detergent. Wait 15 minutes and den rinse.

Part 12

EMERGENCY FIRST-AID

Black Eye	Hold a cold New York strip to da bruised area right after being socked.
Bite	Wash wound wid soap and water. Apply antiseptic den bandage.
Broken Bone	Don't move unless youse have to. Make youself a splint from a piece of wood or use a shot gun.
Bullit Wound	Find a doctor youse can trust.
Burn	Dunk area in cold water. Don't apply grease, leave it alone.
Poison	Dilute wid milk or water. Induce vomiting, only when not a strong acid, alkali, or petroleum. For acid poisoning, neutralize wid milk of magnesia. For alkali poisoning, such as lye or ammonia, give lemon juice or vinegar, den milk. If poison is a sleeping drug, induce vomiting and give strong espresso.
Stab Wound	Apply pressure to stop da bleeding, den clean and bandage.

INDEX

About the Author

Barbara La Rocco, a true Bronx native, was born into a world where crime and justice danced a delicate tango—her father was an NYPD Detective who spent 25 years chasing down organized crime. After snagging a degree in criminal justice at the University of Central Florida, she hit the road, working in glamorous resort towns from Hilton Head to the neon lights of Las Vegas.

Barbara has traded in her mobster tales for coastal crusades. As the founder of the nonprofit Going Coastal, she's on a mission to raise awareness about urban waterfronts and coastal issues—because who says you can't save the planet while stirring up some killer recipes? She's authored guides on urban waterfronts like Going Coastal New York City, as well as reviving classics such as A Maritime History of New York and Around Manhattan's Rim.

While her current focus is on coastal environments, Barbara still keeps her ear to the ground for all things mob-related—after all, whether it's in the kitchen or on the waterfront, she knows how to mix a little intrigue with her passion!

www.ingramcontent.com/pod-product-compliance
Lightning Source LLC
Chambersburg PA
CBHW050958050726
47592CB00007B/2620
* 9 7 8 0 9 7 2 9 8 0 3 4 0 *